# SECRETS IN
# Yellowstone & Grand
# National Parks

Published by National Photographic Collections
North Palm Beach, Florida

2

**SECRETS IN YELLOWSTONE AND GRAND TETON NATIONAL PARKS**
By Lorraine Salem Tufts
*Photographs by* Al Buchanan, Michael Francis, Steven Fuller, C.F. Glover, Jeff Henry, Henry Holdsworth, Brad Markel, Ken McGraw, Sandy Nykerk, Neil & Trish Ramhorst, Robert Smith, Lorraine Salem Tufts
*Published by* National Photographic Collections
*Art Director:* Lorraine Salem Tufts
*Designer:* Katie Pelisek
*Contributing Writers:* Steven Fuller, Tracey I. Holmes, Sandy Nykerk & Zoe Sanders
*Consulting Editor:* Ellen Koteff
*Assisting Editors:* Tracey I. Holmes & Zoe Sanders
*Historical Researcher:* Barbara Brams
*Published in the United States by:*
**National Photographic Collections**
**390 Golfview Road F, North Palm Beach**
**Florida 33408 USA**
**1-800-411-6144**
**1-561-626-3233**
**www.nationalphotocollections.com**
*Printed & Bound:* Regent Publishing
*Typography:* Typo Graphics Inc. Orlando, FL
 Set in: Winsor Light Condensed, Metro
 Black 2, & Berkeley Oldstyle Medium
Printed in China
Eighth Printing
**Softcover**

Fifth Edition
First Edition Copyright © 1988
Second Edition Copyright © 1990
Third Edition Copyright ©1994, 1997
Fourth Edition Copyright © 2002
Fifth Edition Copyright © 2005

National Photographic Collections
**Hardcover**

Fourth Edition
First Edition Copyright © 1990
Second Edition Copyright © 1994, 1997
Third Edition Copyright © 2002
Fourth Edition Copyright © 2005

National Photographic Collections
Library of Congress Cataloging in Publication data
 Tufts, Lorraine Salem, 1947-
  Secrets in Yellowstone & Grand Teton
  National Parks
 1. Yellowstone & Grand Teton Park-
  Description-Photographic.
 I. Tufts, Lorraine Salem   II. Title
  . . 1990   . 90-61150
Secrets in, # 1
ISBN 0-9620255-1-8   Softcover Edition
ISBN 0-9620255-2-6   Hardcover Edition

## Acknowledgements

The author wishes to express her gratitude to the Grand Teton Natural History Association and the Yellowstone Association of Natural Science, History and Education, Inc.

Special thanks go to: Sharlene Milligan, Executive Director of the Grand Teton Natural History Association; Gene Ball, Director of the Yellowstone Association; Timothy Manns, Naturalist & Historian; Bruce Nelson, Professor of Environmental Science at the University of Virginia; Mark Thompson, Steven Fuller, Michael Francis, Henry Holdsworth, Bob Smith, A very special thank you to Barbara Brams, Tracey I. Holmes and my Mother, Sophie M. Salem for their deep commitment and love to me as I struggled with various aspects of this project over the years. Thanks to: Tracey I. Holmes & Zoe Sanders for their historical and literary input; to Katie Pelisek, Roger Burnard, Greg Tate, Rosanna Griffin, Anne & Buford Potts, Mary Lou Edgley, Clifford Brokaw, Katie Duffy, Hugh Lane, Warren & Jeff Brams, Penelope Edwards, Jim Fenstermaker, Clyde Hall, Donald Pharr and last but not least Marguerite I. Holmes for their helpful assistance. I would like to thank Josh Thompson for the all night graphics when I need it. I thank my Mother and Father for their instant generosity and encouragement.

## Credits

Contributing writers are Tracey I. Holmes and Zoe Sanders, page 57. Steven Fuller, photo descriptions, page 2, 27 & 45. Sandy Nykerk, page 12 & 43.

The quote on page 90 and the information on page 90 and 91, is taken from William H. Romme and Don G. Despain in their article, "The Yellowstone Fires," Scientific American, November 1989, Volume 261, Number 5, pages 37-46 with the author's and publisher's permission.

*Lorraine Salem Tufts*                *Canon EOS 5*
*300 2.8Lens,1/500 at f5.6*        *Fuji Provia 100*
**B L A C K   B E A R   C U B**

*Lorraine Salem Tufts*                *Canon EOS 5*
*300 2.8Lens, 1/500 at f6.7*       *Fuji Provia 100*
**F E M A L E**
**G R I Z Z L Y   B E A R**

*Cover Photographs* by Lorraine Salem Tufts, **FALL SUNSET**, 20-35mmLens,1/6sec. at f16, Tripod, Kodachrome 25. **GREAT FOUNTAIN GEYSER**, 20-35mmLens,1/10sec. at f16, Tripod, Fujichrome 100. **FEMALE GRIZZLY BEAR**, 300mm2.8Lens,1/500sec. at f6.7 Fuji Provia 100. **GRAND TETON RANGE FROM OXBOW BEND**, 24mmLens,1/15 sec. at f16, Polarizer, Tripod, Kodachrome 25

*Title Page Photographs:* **DANCING FOXES** *by Steven Fuller, Nikon F3 with Motor Drive, Nikkor 180mm Lens, 1/250sec. at f5.6,Kodachrome 64*
A mated pair taken in late February. Such postures are associated with mating season. They stood in this position for six to eight seconds before breaking apart. The foxes appeared in the central area of Yellowstone.

To youth that has the courage to strive for high ideals, contra mundum.

*Lorraine Salem Tufts, Canon F1, Canon 80-200mm Zoom Lens, 1/250 sec. at f5.6, 64 Kodachrome.*

## MULE DEER FAWN

4

*Robert H. Smith    Nikon F3    Nikkor 50mm Lens, 1/2 sec. at f16    Gitzo Tripod    25 Kodachrome*

### ELECTRIC PEAK AT SUNRISE

The secret of this photograph is the perfect moment of morning light from Swan Lake Flat. Patience and a keen eye allowed the photographer to seize the foreground, middle-ground and background with exceptional clarity. The mountain, Electric Peak, dominates the landscape at 10,992 feet above sea level, in Yellowstone National Park.

*Neil and Trish Ramhorst*      *Nikon FE2 with Motor Drive*      *Nikkor 400mm 3.5 Lens, 1/125 at f3.5*      *Gitzo Tripod*      *64 Kodachrome*

**BULL ELK WITH COW IN THE MORNING MIST**

6

*Lorraine Salem Tufts*　　　　　　　*Canon EOS 2AE*　　　　　　　*Canon 20-35 mm Lens, 1/2 sec. at f22*
*Bogen Tripod*　　　　　　　*Polarizing Filter*　　　　　　　*Fuji Velvia 50*

## M O U N T   M O R A N   A T   S U N S E T

Mount Moran and the Snake River at OxBow Bend during sunset are an awe-inspiring sight.
This mountain stands 12,605 feet above sea level and renders a majestic landscape from
Jackson Lake Lodge, Oxbow Bend and Moran Junction.

# Introduction

Yellowstone National Parks is located in the northwestern corner of Wyoming with its borders extending north and northwest into Montana and west into Idaho. Directly south lies Grand Teton National Park. Federal law protects and preserves the natural evolution of the geology, fauna, and flora in both parks for the "enjoyment of present and future generations."

The Greater Yellowstone Ecosystem is comprised of national forests, refuges and other federal, state and privately owned lands.

We present a collection of photographs and information about the area. Thirteen photographers exhibit 145 photographs of animals, scenics, wildfire and familiar natural phenomena. They also share secrets on how they created these pictures.

Most members of this photographic group live in the area or are frequent visitors, maintaining the constant data required for capturing certain difficult images. Years of studying the light, animals and environment with patience, curiosity, creativity and respect produced this photographic collection. Most cases of ethical photographic behavior require distance. Large, fast telephoto lenses contribute to wildlife photography by magnifying and thereby offering comfortable and necessary distances for the animals. Sometimes photographers cross country ski or hike to remote places where they examine signs of wildlife. After checking the lighting, they set-up near a tree or river for the better part of a day, virtually unnoticed by passing animals. It is important to exhibit great patience and stealth, especially when rare photo opportunities present themselves. Feeding animals and setting up a constructed blind are prohibited in the parks, making a knowledge of the area and the species a critical tool gained only after years of work.

**Secrets in Yellowstone and Grand Teton National Parks** offers an opportunity to own a cameoed collection of breathtaking scenics, wildlife species in their habitat and splendid hydrothermal images.

*Lorraine Salem Tufts*
*Canon 150-600mm 5.6 Lens, 1/500 sec. at f5.6*          *Bogen Tripod*          *Canon T -90*
*64 Kodachrome*

P A I R   O F   T R U M P E T E R   S W A N S

8

*Lorraine Salem Tufts*     *Canon EOS A2E*     *Canon 35-350mm 3.5-5.6Lens, 1/2sec. at f16*     *Bogen Tripod*     *Fuji Velvia 50*

### SUNRISE OVER THE ABSAROKA RANGE AND YELLOWSTONE LAKE

The word Absaroka is Native American for the Crow Nation. It means "bird people"or "children of the large beaked bird". Other interpretations also refer to birds. Most of the eastern boundary of Yellowstone is flanked by the mountain range. With a little imagination one might see the silhouette of a "sleeping giant" looking skyward from the configuration of various mountains such as Castor and Pollux.

# Yellowstone National Park

*Lorraine Salem Tufts*
*Canon 35-105mm Zoom Lens, 1/1000 sec. at f22,*  *Polarizer*   *Canon AE1 Program*
*64 Kodachrome*

## OLD FAITHFUL
### DURING SUNRISE IN THE FALL

Old Faithful is the most famous geyser in Yellowstone National Park. Appropriately named by General Henry D. Washburn in 1870, this geyser continues to erupt at fairly regular intervals. At times it reaches the extraordinary height of 180 feet.

*Lorraine Salem Tufts*
*Canon 300mm Lens, 1/250sec. at f8*

*Canon EOS A2E*
*100 Fujichrome*

**A YOUNG MALE ELK LOOKS CLOSELY AT
A YEARLING AS SHE RESTS ON OPAL
TERRACE, MAMMOTH HOT SPRINGS**

*Lorraine Salem Tufts*
*Canon 35-105mm Lens, 1/30 sec. at f16*

*Polarizer, Monopod*

*Canon AE1 Program*
*64 Kodachrome*

**FISHING CONE, YELLOWSTONE LAKE AND
THE ABSAROKA MOUNTAINS AS VIEWED
FROM THE WEST THUMB GEYSER BASIN**

# Hot Springs & The Hot Spot

Hot springs are a phenomena often characteristic of a recently active volcanic area. They are a point of release for underground water which has been heated by magma or molten rock. The water temperature is at least 10-15°F (6-9°C) warmer than the air temperature of the area. These springs may represent the last stage of heat loss by molten or partly molten material found beneath the Earth's surface. While slowly cooling, igneous rock gives off high temperature vapors and gases.

Geysers and fumaroles are usually found in volcanic areas. A geyser is a hot water spring which periodically erupts into a fountain. A fumarole is a point of release for fumes and gases. All three, hot springs, geysers and fumaroles, are places where volcanically-heated water escapes. The source of water for geysers and fumaroles is primarily snow and rain. This water, guided by gravity, seeps down cracks, cavities, passages, and tunnels within the hardening level below the thermal area and is heated.

Geysers (from Icelandic "Geysa") discharge ground water heated to the boiling point by extremely hot rocks. Ground water, when held in a chamber and brought to a boiling point below the surface, will violently force out a column of water above it. Consequently, geysers erupt in periodic jets of water and steam. To see the geyser's rapid rush of water, there must be a crack which extends upward and opens at the Earth's surface. After the eruption, the long, narrow opening or fissure fills again with relatively cold ground water, the water heats, and the phenomenon begins again. Many hot springs erupt with regularity—some show periods of violent boiling while others alternately discharge water and gas.

Fountain geysers and cone geysers are the two types of geysers found in Yellowstone. Geyserite, which holds the overflow of water in a pool, forms a basin. A column of water can burst through the pool to create a fountain geyser. Cone geysers have a buildup of geyserite deposits that eventually form the cone

around the mouth of the geyser. Higher temperature thermal springs may contain silica which can precipitate and form geyserite cones and terraces.

Fumaroles (from Latin fumus, "smoke") are steam vents. Acidic gases such as hydrogen sulfide and carbon dioxide are typically present. Because the water supply is limited in fumaroles and because temperatures can easily vary, the temperature of a fumarole can fluctuate enormously over time. Solfataras (Italian *Zolfa,* "sulfur") are fumaroles with sulfurous gases. Paint pots, mud pots, and mud volcanoes are also fumaroles. They have a limited water supply and an acidic response. The mud comes from the chemical attack by steam and acidic gases on the surface of the rocks. In addition, the iron present in these rocks gives them a painted look.

Travertine terraces are a form of limestone or calcium carbonate. The hot spring water carries dissolved calcium carbonate held in solution by the high temperature and by the

*Lorraine Salem Tufts, Canon T-90, Canon 35-105mm Lens, 1/125 sec. at f8, Tripod, 25 Kodachrome.*

**CHOCOLATE POT
ON THE GIBBON RIVER**

dissolved carbon dioxide. Upon cooling at the surface and losing carbon dioxide, the calcium carbonate precipitates as travertine, which slowly builds terraces such as those found at Mammoth Hot Springs.

Pools are hot springs that do not erupt. They are also formed from the geyserite, but because of their shape, discharge heat by boiling on the surface.

The last of three major eruptions of the Yellowstone hot spot occurred 600,000 years ago. The eruption involving two catastrophic explosions created a large caldera—a relatively oval, basin-shaped volcanic depression—measuring 45 miles long and 27 miles wide. For thousands of years, the lava flow that followed these eruptions formed a magnificent and varied landscape. Most of the geyser basins are in the caldera, as are Lewis Lake, Shoshone Lake, the northern part of Yellowstone Lake, Hayden Valley, and parts of the Yellowstone River.

Subterranean heat, which keeps the park thermally active, may still have other stories to tell. In the larger picture, the Yellowstone hot spot, mentioned above, is thought to be a volcanic plume rising from deep below the Earth's surface. It may be 60 to 120 miles wide and may have been active a minimum of tens of millions of years.

The Earth is not yet middle-aged by the accounts of many geologists. This restless hot spot and all her crowning hot springs have many more dramatic days and nights. For 5 billion more years, the Earth's surface will cool, shift, crack, erupt, split, explode, and sink.

It is estimated that there are as many as 10,000 thermal features in Yellowstone National Park, making this park the largest hydrothermal area on Earth. It is difficult to imagine Yellowstone as a more diverse, more beautiful, or more mysterious place. It is also difficult to imagine it as completely devastated, as has happened before. Whatever the future brings, visiting and seeing Yellowstone is one of the great gifts of our age.

12

*Sandy Nykerk*          *Nikon FE2*          *Nikkor 24mm Lens, 1/60 sec. at f8*          *Polarizer*          *Bogen Tripod*          *64 Kodachrome*

### SUNSET AT THE LOWER GEYSER BASIN

The sun setting behind the steam plume from Clepsydra Geyser in the Lower Geyser Basin and a dramatic cloud bank contribute to an "other world" effect in this photograph. By scouting locations and anticipating the light, a photographer can greatly enhance the probability of being well positioned.

# Man's History In Yellowstone

Because of the determination of a few outstanding men, a geographically isolated area in the Northwestern wilderness of the United States is recognized as one of the nation's most valuable resources for natural phenomenon. This area, called Yellowstone National Park, began receiving public attention as a result of the awe-inspiring photographs, sketches, and descriptive essays from Dr. Ferdinand Hayden's expedition in 1871. Specifically, the photography of William Henry Jackson and the artwork of Thomas Moran inspired congressmen to push through legislation that would preserve Yellowstone for all generations.

Native Americans, the first people acquainted with Yellowstone, had great respect for the spirits that made thunderous noises where the Earth trembles and water boils with smoke. The Crow, Blackfeet, Shoshoni, and Bannock are all credited with knowledge of the area, but it is thought they were infrequent visitors.

One Native American tribe, the *Tukudikas*, did permanently inhabit the area. For their sustenance, they hunted bighorn sheep with horn bows. By all accounts of white trappers and hunters, they were without horses. Osborne Russell, a trapper, observed them as timid, small people living in fear of aggressive outsiders.

By the 1840s, the Northern Shoshoni and Bannock Tribes were forced to visit the country of Yellowstone in an annual search for bison. Their normal herds were disappearing from the Snake River plains.

In 1804, Thomas Jefferson sent explorers Lewis and Clark into the recently acquired territory of the Louisiana Purchase. Although they never entered Yellowstone, a member of their expedition, John C. Colter, did. By 1807 and 1808, his familiarity with the natives and fur trading took his search for new business into the thermal areas, and he is credited as being the first white man to witness geysers and cauldrons. His verbal accounts of Lake Yellowstone were later used on a map by William Clark.

In the 1820s and 1830s, other fur traders entered the region. Daniel T. Potts, overwhelmed by what he saw, wrote the first published description of Yellowstone.

According to historian Aubrey Haines, the acting governor of the Montana Territory, Thomas Francis Meagher, suggested in 1865 that this land should be placed aside for all to see and enjoy.

Finally, in 1869, Nathaniel Langford, a Montana resident and later the park's first superintendent, organized the first Yellowstone expedition. Included were David E. Folsom, Charles E. Cook, and William Peterson. These men were greatly affected by the

*Lorraine Salem Tufts, Canon F1 with Motor Drive, Canon 150-600mm 5.6 Lens, 1/250 sec. at f11, Gitzo Tripod, Slik Pro Ball Head, 64 Kodachrome.*

**BULL MOOSE AT SUNRISE**

abundance of natural wonders in the region. Folsom suggested the area be kept free of settlers so everyone could appreciate it as he had.

In 1870, Langford convinced Henry D. Washburn, Surveyor General of Montana, to lead a second expedition into Yellowstone. This expedition brought stories of the Grand Canyon, Lake Yellowstone, and the geyser basins to influential Montana residents. Washburn's party agreed that this land should be preserved. Langford traveled East with his lectures on the uniqueness of the area.

One year later, in 1871, Dr. Ferdinand Hayden of the United States Geological Survey organized a government-backed expedition that included both biologists and land surveyors. More importantly, however, this expedition was unique in that it included among its explorers a photographer William H. Jackson. Also included was the artist Thomas Moran. Their combined artwork brought to the world the natural wonders of Yellowstone and enabled those people who had never seen the area to visualize and therefore appreciate its beauty. The language of pictures helped preserve the area's natural phenomenon by inspiring politicians to advocate laws which would permanently safeguard this environment against future encroachment and exploitation. Finally, in 1872, President Ulysses S. Grant signed a bill passed by the Congress which made government protection of Yellowstone National Park lawful; thus it became the world's first national park.

In 1879, a government headquarters was erected in Mammoth and $10,000 in government funds was provided to protect the land and wildlife from such threats as Indian hunters and white poachers. However, it was not until 1916 that the National Park Service was created. Today, it provides tireless service to the public, the maintenance of the park, research, protection of the natural inhabitants—in fact, the list goes on and on. The National Park Service exercises constant flexibility as geological, ecological, and political circumstances and public information change.

*Lorraine Salem Tufts, Canon EOS 5, Canon 35-350mm Lens, 1/500 sec. at f5.6, 100 Fuji Provia*

### FEMALE GRIZZLY BEAR FEEDING HER CUBS

Cubs are usually weaned in the second year during the spring after their winter sleep. This may be one of the last times these cubs feed from mother on this May afternoon.

*Lorraine Salem Tufts        Canon EOS 5        Canon 35-350mm Lens        1/250 sec.at f5.6        1/125 sec. at f5.6        100 Fuji Provia*

### GRIZZLY BEAR FEEDING ON CARRION

It took over and hour for the large grizzly bear to negotiate the fast flowing water of LeHardys Rapids. When finally it made its way to the bison remains, it slowly looked around, licked its chops and began feeding. Visitors from the world over witnessed this interesting natural phenomenon. After feeding on the carcass for quite awhile the bear stopped, looked in the direction from which it came, entered the rapids and left going the same way. It was most enjoyable watching the grizzly think through the entire endeavor.

*Lorraine Salem Tufts*          *Canon EOS 5*          *Canon 600mm 4. Lens, 1/350sec. at f6.7*          *Tripod*          *100 Fuji Provia*

## FEMALE GRIZZLY BEAR WITH TWO YEAR OLD CUBS
Grizzly bears feed on a wide range of plant and animal food, such as berries, pine nuts, grasses, clovers, forbs, rodents, rabbits, large mammals and carrion just to name several. Cubs learn how to hunt and where to find these foods from their mother in about two years. They are capable of supporting themselves in that time and can survive on their own.

16

*Lorraine Salem Tufts*       *Canon EOS A2E*       *Canon 35-350mm 3.5-5.6Lens, 1/90 sec at f5.6*       *Fuji Sensia 100*

## COYOTE HUNTING FOR RODENTS ON A COLD WINTER'S DAY

Coyotes are animals to respect. They have a great ability to adapt to whatever obstacles man or nature poses. Often coyotes are afraid of people, and rightfully so, for they have been hunted extensively. In Yellowstone, as in the Grand Tetons, they are left to their own destiny, unharmed by humans. It was very exciting capturing this moment on film, because of the stark blanket of snow and the lone coyote. These two subjects contribute to an unusual composition in nature. Often trees, grass, tracks, or other objects detract from the simple beauty of the photograph.

*Ken McGraw*          *Nikon F3 with Motor Drive*          *Nikkor 600mm Lens, 1/125 sec. at f5.6*          *Tripod*          *64 Kodachrome*

## BOBCAT WITH PREY

Solitary and secretive, the bobcat is rarely seen because it dwells in inaccessible rocky terrain with dense cover. These animals possess keen senses and are known to be proficient hunters. Bobcats prefer to stalk and then leap or pounce on their prey. While not a common sight in the park, this species is part of the Greater Yellowstone Ecosystem.

| *Neil and Trish Ramhorst* | *Nikon FE2 with Motor Drive* | *Nikkor 300mm Lens, 1/250 sec. at f8* | *Gitzo Tripod* | *64 Kodachrome* |

## FEMALE BADGER WITH THREE YOUNG

Stealth, patience and a long telephoto lens were the tools needed to capture this rare sight. After numerous hikes in Lamar Valley, these photographers found a female badger in the den with her young. After hours of waiting, mother emerged, looked around, and then allowed her three young to come out and play in the sunlight.

*Robert H. Smith*          *Nikon F3*          *Nikkor 24mm Lens, 16 sec. at f5.6*          *Gitzo Tripod*          *25 Kodachrome*

## MOONRISE AT MAMMOTH TERRACES

Taken from Mammoth Hot Springs, this scene shows a small thermal spring with dead trees from the hot water overflow. This, along with the moon and Mount Everts, sets the stage for a beautiful composition. Here the photographer's secret is the constant study of the area and the ever-changing beauty caused by temperature, light, and weather. A compromise was necessary to provide adequate depth of field and still freeze the motion of the moon.

20

*Lorraine Salem Tufts*
*Canon 35-350 mm Lens, 1/60 sec at f5.6*

*Canon EOS 5*
*Fuji Provia100*

## HERE THEY COME!

*Lorraine Salem Tufts*
*Canon 35-350 mm Lens, 1/60 sec. at f5.6*

*Canon EOS 5*
*Fuji Provia100*

## THERE THEY GO!

Three playful bison calves amused on-lookers as they romped on the road. The adult females flanked the young ones as they moved. Only after the adults separated them did they settle down and cross.

*Lorraine Salem Tufts     Canon F1 with Motor Drive     Canon 150-600mm 5.6 Zoom Lens, 1/250 sec. at f5.6     Gitzo Tripod, Slik Pro Ball Head     64 Kodachrome*

## YOUNG BULLS SPARRING DURING THE RUT

These bison are young bulls that belong to a herd of twelve or thirteen cows, calves and yearlings. This display is more an exercise in combat than an actual battle, yet it provides action for an exciting photograph with the advantage being the wait and a long lens.

22

*Lorraine Salem Tufts*          *Canon F1 with Motor Drive*          *Canon 35-105mm 3.5 Zoom Lens, 1/125 sec. at f16*          *64 Kodachrome*

## BULL, COW AND A CALF

A beautiful morning in August provided excellent lighting for this photograph of bison along the Yellowstone River in Hayden Valley. To enhance the image, back lighting was used so the bison would appear dark and silhouetted in front of the river. The passing ducks add further intrigue to this scene.

An artistic approach to picture taking usually adds a romantic aspect to the portrayal of the subject matter.

*Lorraine Salem Tufts*
*Canon 80-200mm 4.0 Zoom Lens, 1/125 sec. at f16*

*Canon F1*
*64 Kodachrome*

## THE LOWER FALLS OF THE YELLOWSTONE RIVER

This awesome 308-foot waterfall can be seen at the Grand Canyon of the Yellowstone. "Piere Jaune" (Yellowstone) came from the early French trappers who fostered this name from the Minnetaree Sioux Indian's term "Mi-tsi-a-da-zi" (Rock Yellow Water).

24

*Henry H. Holdsworth*                    *Nikon FE2 with Motor Drive*
*Nikkor 400mm Lens, 1/250 sec. at f8*      *Gitzo Tripod*      *64 Kodachrome*

### BULL MOOSE AFTER SHEDDING VELVET

Moose are the largest members of the deer family. Only the males bear antlers, and they use them to compete with other males during the rut.

For three weeks, this photographer followed a herd of bulls. They finally began shedding velvet by rubbing their antlers against the trees. After another long wait this bull came out of the woods in the evening light to feed on willows. There were still a few strands of velvet hanging from his antlers.

*Lorraine Salem Tufts*                                    *Canon F1 with Motor Drive*
                *Canon 150-600mm 5.6 Zoom Lens, 1/500 sec. at f8*
*Gitzo Tripod with Slik Pro Ball Head*                          *200 Kodachrome*

## COW MOOSE FEEDING ON AQUATIC PLANTS

Moose wade into streams and ponds, submerging their heads to reach the roots and stems of aquatic plants. Animals in the wild often select a diet which achieves an optimal balance between energy intake and the requirements for certain nutrients such as sodium.

*Henry H. Holdsworth*          *Cambo SCII*          *Nikkor 135mm Lens, 1/30 sec. at f32 1/2*          *Gitzo Tripod*          *Ektachrome 100 Professional*

## CANARY SPRING AT MAMMOTH HOT SPRINGS
A sunrise in April illuminates these travertine terraces and displays colors from algae and bacteria.

*Steven Fuller*      *Nikon F3, with Motor Drive*      *Nikkor 200mm Lens, 1/125 sec. at f4*      *64 Kodachrome*

### BULL ELK TÊTE À TÊTE
Although the rut was over, these two bulls were sparring a hard-fought match for no other purpose than the endless jousting for social dominance typical of hooved animals.

*Jeff Henry*      *Nikon F3*      *Nikkor 85mm Lens, 1/250 sec. at f2.8*      *64 Kodachrome*

## BULL ELK SHEDDING HIS VELVET

The fuzzy vascular skin on the antlers of the bull elk is called velvet. After five months, a mature bull can have a five-foot rack weighing as much as thirty pounds. By mid-August the velvet dries and is rubbed off by the bull, exposing the horny antler underneath.

*C.F. Glover*                                  *Canon F1 with Motor Drive*
*Bogen Tripod*      *Canon 400mm Lens, 1.4 x Extender, 1/250 sec. at f5.6*      *64 Kodachrome*

## COW ELK WITH NEWBORN FEMALE CALF

Elk usually begin calving at the end of May. This cow recently gave birth to this wobbly-legged calf. The calf is trying to follow its mother while steadying itself in the shallow water. Amazingly, calves begin walking soon after birth. This sequence of photographs stirs one's imagination and curiosity as to the communication between the pair.

30

*Lorraine Salem Tufts*          *Canon T-90*          *Canon 35-105mm Lens, 1/20 at f22*          *Bogen Tripod*          *25 Kodachrome*

## MINERVA TERRACE AT MAMMOTH HOT SPRINGS
Travertine, a finely crystalline and massive deposit of calcium carbonate known as limestone, displays the white, tan, and cream colors of the terrace. This, along with the colors from living organisms such as algae and bacteria which grow in the warm waters, create the spectacular natural phenomenon known as Minerva Terrace.

*Lorraine Salem Tufts*
*Canon 150-600mm 5.6 Zoom Lens, 1/250 sec. at f8*

*Canon F1 with Motor Drive*
*Gitzo Tripod          64 Kodachrome*

## YOUNG MALE PRONGHORN ANTELOPE

This ungulate is the only animal in the world that sheds its horns as though they were antlers. Both males and females have horns. The male's horns are larger and have more curl. The bony core is permanent, while the outer horny sheath is shed in November or December. The females have horns most of the time, but they are much smaller than the males and are not shed.

**32**

*Lorraine Salem Tufts*                                                        *Canon T-90*
*Canon 300mm 2.8 Lens, 1/250 sec. at f8*        *Velbon Monopod*        *64 Kodachrome*

### BIGHORN SHEEP RAM
During the rut, rams will vie for dominance in the mating ritual by ramming horns and heads with great force.

*Lorraine Salem Tufts*                                                        *Canon T-90*
*Canon 300mm Lens, 1/250 sec. at f8*        *Velbon Monopod*        *64 Kodachrome*

### BIGHORN SHEEP EWE
The horns of ewes are shorter and a great deal thinner than those of rams.

*Lorraine Salem Tufts      Canon F1 with Motor Drive      Canon 150-600mm Zoom Lens, 1/125 sec. at f5.6      Gitzo Tripod with Slik Pro Ball Head      64 Kodachrome*

## MULE DEER IN VELVET

At the time this buck was photographed, it was traveling in a bachelor herd of three. Its antlers are almost full grown in this late July picture. The buck will rub off its velvet by September and shed its antlers well after the rut in late January or early February.

**34**

*Lorraine Salem Tufts, Canon T-90, Canon 300mm 2.8 Lens, 1/250 sec. at f8, Monopod, 64 Kodachrome.*

**B I G H O R N   S H E E P   L A M B**

*Henry H. Holdsworth, Nikon FE2 with Motor Drive, Nikkor 400mm Lens, 1/60 sec. at f5.6 Gitzo Tripod, 64 Kodachrome.*

**P R O N G H O R N
A N T E L O P E   F A W N**

*Lorraine Salem Tufts, Canon F1 with Motor Drive, Canon 80-200mm Lens, 1/250 sec. at f5.6, 64 Kodachrome.*

**M U L E   D E E R   F A W N**

*Lorraine Salem Tufts*  *Canon T-90*
*Velbon Monopod*  *Canon 300mm 2.8 Lens, 1/180 sec. at f4*  *100 Fujichrome*

**E L K   C A L F**

*Henry H. Holdsworth*  *Nikon FE2*
*Nikkor 400mm Lens, 1/125 sec. at f4*  *Gitzo Tripod*  *64 Kodachrome*

**B I S O N   C A L F**

*Jeff Henry*          *Nikon F3*          *Nikkor 35mm 2.8 Lens, 1/250 sec. at f22*          *64 Kodachrome*

### OLD FAITHFUL AT SUNRISE
In this photograph Old Faithful erupts while all is still at the Old Faithful Inn. Every distracting color and shape is covered under a blanket of snow. The snow is illuminated by the golden glow of the early morning sun. The world seems perfect at this moment in this place.

*Lorraine Salem Tufts*    *Canon EOS 5*    *Canon 20-35mm 3.5-4.5Lens, 1/10 sec. at f16*    *Polarizer*    *Bogan Tripod*    *100 Fuji Provia*

## OPALESCENT POOL IN BLACK SAND BASIN

Opalescent means, "having a milky iridescence." The blue color of the pool reflects this when the sun is brightly shining overhead. The rusty orange hues around the pool are algae and bacteria living under a shield of warm water runoff. The "bobbi sox" trees also add interest to the picture. The name originates from the white trunks which formed when mineral-rich runoff from the hot springs invades the area. The trees draw the mineral-rich water into their trunks causing them to eventually die.

*Michael H. Francis*          *Canon F1 with Motor Dirve*          *Canon 500mm 4.5 Lens, 1/250 sec. at f5.6*          *Bogen Tripod*          *64 Kodachrome*

## RIVER OTTERS

River otters are secretive and seldom seen in the rivers of Yellowstone. This mother and her young pup are playing and fishing in the Lamar River. Often river otters will energetically shake the water from their fur, creating a circular spray of water as shown in this photograph.

38

*Henry H. Holdsworth*                                                                 *Nikon FM*
*Nikkor 55mm Lens, 1/15 sec. at f32     Locking Cable Release     Gitzo Tripod     25 Kodachrome*

## LIGHTNING IN HAYDEN VALLEY

Hayden Valley lies in the caldera, an enormous basin-shaped depression, caused by a volcanic explosion about 600,000 years ago.

Lightning shots look best when foreground is included. It is easier to photograph at night when longer exposures catch the flashes. For day or night, point the lens at the heaviest concentration of lightning and focus on infinity. Set the aperture high and the shutter speed slow using a locking cable release. This photographer let his meter guide his exposure, and he kept shooting until he caught the lightning streaking across the sky.

*Al Buchanan     Olympus OM1     50mm Zuiko Lens, 1/125 sec. at f16     Tripod     64 Kodachrome*

## PETRIFIED TREES ON SPECIMEN RIDGE

Specimen Ridge is home to one of Yellowstone's most unique natural wonders: a petrified forest with a number of the trees left standing vertically in groups. These trees were fossilized after being covered by an enormous fall of volcanic ash. With the passing of centuries, the forest re-established itself, the mountains erupted again, and this chain of events continued possibly 5 or 6 times, giving rise to the theory that multiple layers actually exist.

Some of the deciduous tall timber that stood here about 50 million years ago were oak, walnut, magnolia, redwood, sycamore, and hickory.

*Lorraine Salem Tufts*
*Canon 35-105mm Lens, 1/180 sec. at f9.5*

*Canon T-90*
*100 Fujichrome*

## TOWER FALLS

Rapidly running water flows over a vertical cliff from Tower Creek, creating the 132-foot drop known as Tower Falls. A mist billows up from the splashing water below, creating a rainbow with the assistance of the morning sunshine. Tower Falls was named for the obelisk volcanic rock formations that flank the creek.

40

*Lorraine Salem Tufts          Canon EOS A2E          Canon 20-35mm 3.5-4.5Lens, 1/15 sec. at f22          Polarizer          Bogen Tripod          Fuji Velvia 50*

## MORNING GLORY POOL

The funnel-shaped blue center of this geothermal, which resembles the corolla of the flower, inspired its namers in the 1880s. Over the years the water temperature has declined, due in part to debris tossed into the pool. Cooler runoff water has caused algae growth, creating the yellow and burnt orange colors around the opening. Greater knowledge and respect for the geothermals contribute to behavior that preserves rather than destroys their unique qualities.

*Lorraine Salem Tufts*      *Canon EOS 5*      *Canon 20-35mm 3.5-4.5 Lens, 1sec. at f22*      *Bogen Tripod*      *25Kodachrome*

## GREAT FOUNTAIN GEYSER ERUPTING AFTER SUNSET

Witnessing Great Fountain Geyser erupting during and after sunset is a premier geothermal experience in Yellowstone. It erupts occasionally during a twenty-four hour period, most often in the dark, during foul weather or harsh afternoon sunlight. The official prediction for this eruption was midday. Seven hours later the geyser erupted displaying four distinct burst of hot water shooting high in the sky, lasting five to seven minutes each. The total eruption activity lasted over forty-five minutes during a beautiful sunset.

*Lorraine Salem Tufts*
*Canon 35-350mm 3.5-5.6Lens, 1/350 sec. at f8*

*Canon EOS A2E*
*Fuji Velvia 50*

## RIVERSIDE GEYSER

Old Faithful may be more famous, but Riverside is more predictable. Located on the bank of the Firehole River, this geyser erupts with a 75-foot slanted column of water over the river.

| | | | | |
|---|---|---|---|---|
| *Sandy Nykerk* | *Nikon FE2* | *Nikkor 24mm Lens, 1/8 sec. at f22* | *Polarizer* | *Bogen Tripod* | *25Kodachrome* |
| *Lorraine Salem Tufts* | *Canon EOS 5* | *Canon 20-35mm Lens, 1/125 at f9.5* | | *Bogen Tripod* | *50 Fuji Velvia* |

## GRAND PRISMATIC SPRING WITH WHIRLPOOL

Found in the Midway Geyser Basin at over 370 feet in diameter, this hot spring, the largest in Yellowstone, discharges about 560 gallons of water per minute. The brilliant blue of the pool is surrounded by concentric circles of colonies of colorful cyanobacteria creating the effect of a giant circular prism. Direct lighting and a polarizing filter to remove the glare from the water are essential to reproduce the luminous colors.

44

*Jeff Henry*                    *Nikon F3*                    *Nikkor 35mm Lens, 1/15 sec. at f22*                    *64 Kodachrome*

### CASTLE GEYSER ERUPTING IN THE WINTER

This geyser was named by the Langford-Doane Expedition in 1870. The sinter cone is almost twelve feet high with a diameter of twenty feet wide across the top. It erupts at approximately nine hour intervals. In this photograph the bison gather at the Upper Geyser. Basin for warmth from the harsh winter temperatures.

*Steven Fuller*  *Nikon F3 with Motor Drive*  *Nikkor 200mm Lens, 1/125 sec. at f11*  *64 Kodachrome*

### ERMINE

In winter, weasels are known as ermine because their fur changes color. Indicative of seasons in transition, the ermine's pelage has changed from summer yellow-brown to stark white. In mid-October, the grasses of the hillside are sun-cured and rimed in frost. Within a week or two, the first of the permanent snows will have covered the meadows, and the ermine will blend perfectly into a snow-capped landscape.

46

*Lorraine Salem Tufts*             *Canon T-90*
*Canon 300mm 2.8 Lens, 1/250 sec. at f8*
*Velbon Monopod*             *64 Kodachrome*

**GOLDEN MANTLED
GROUND SQUIRREL**

*Lorraine Salem Tufts*             *Canon T-90*
*Canon 300mm 2.8 Lens with 1.4 Converter, 1/500 sec. at f5.6*
*Velbon Monopod*             *100 Fujichrome*

**LEAST CHIPMUNK**

*Lorraine Salem Tufts*             *Pentax 90WR 200m*
*90mm Automatic Focus*
*Flash*             *100 Fujichrome*

**RED SQUIRREL**

*Trish Ramhorst*             *Nikon FE2 with Motor Drive*
*Nikkor 300mm 4.5 Lens, 1/125 sec. at f11*
*Gitzo Tripod*             *64 Kodachrome*

**YELLOWBELLY MARMOT
YAWNING**

*Lorraine Salem Tufts*        *Canon EOS 5*        *Canon 28-105 mm Lens, 1/250 sec. at f11*        *Fuji Provia100*

### LONE STAR GEYSER ERUPTING WITH A DOUBLE RAINBOW

Lone Star Geyser is located about 3.5 miles from Old Faithful. Take the Lone Star trailhead, located just south of Kepler Cascades. The 2.3 mile hike is a pleasant, easy hike and well worth the effort as you can see.

48

*Michael H. Francis*                                          *Canon F1 with Motor Drive*
*Canon 300mm Lens, 1/125 sec. at f5.6*            *Bogen Tripod*            *64 Kodachrome*

## BOREAL OWL

Generally a very docile creature, the small boreal owl is known for its large head. The owl ranges in size from approximately 8½ to 12 inches. A pesky raven revealed the owl to the photographer, making this photograph possible. Yellowstone National Park records indicate this 1986 encounter was the first confirmed sighting of a boreal owl in the park.

*Lorraine Salem Tufts*          *Canon* EOS A2E          *Canon 300mm 2.8Lens, 1/500 sec. at 5.6*          *Tripod with Wimberly Head Mount*          *100 Fujichrome*

## BALD EAGLE IN FLIGHT

Eagles are the champion visual animals on Earth, having the ability to spot their prey two miles away. Bald eagles are equipped with muscles in their eyes that control lens curvature. This makes them capable of an accurate preception of movement on the ground throughout their flight and dive. They also have an extra eyelid called a nictitating membrane, which is used to clean and protect their eyes.

Bald Eagles can measure up to seven feet, wing-tip to wing-tip, and weigh as much as fourteen pounds. They primarily live on fish, but are known to eat ducks, rodents, and carrion.

*Lorraine Salem Tufts*        *Canon T-90*        *Canon 150-600mm 5.6 Lens, 1/500 sec. at f9.5*        *Tripod*        *100 Fujichrome*

## OSPREY LEAPING FROM THE NEST

Osprey catch fish exclusively. They must be careful not to catch fish that are too large for them to bring out of the water. Once their talons clamp on the fish and they start their lift, their legs extend, and this locks their talons onto the prey. It is impossible to release the fish at this point. Their feet have tiny spicules (or spines) on them contributing to a good hold.

*Lorraine Salem Tufts*                                                         *Canon F1 with Motor Drive*
*Canon 600mm Lens, 1/250 sec. at f5.6*          *Bogen Tripod*                 *64 Kodachrome*

## GREAT GRAY OWL

Mysterious is the word best used to describe the great gray owl. This raptor measures two feet or more in height with a wing span of approximately five feet. It is the largest owl in North America, and is extremely difficult to spot because it flies silently and blends well with the forest. Being predominantly nocturnal, this daylight photograph is especially rare.

**52**

*Lorraine Salem Tufts*      *Canon EOS A2E*      *Canon 600mm 4Lens, 1/500 sec. at f 5.6*      *Bogen Tripod, with Wimberly Mount*      *Fuji Provia 100*

### SANDHILL CRANE IN FLIGHT

Sandhill cranes are very large birds. Standing at about three feet with a wing-span of between six and seven feet. They are awesome to witness in flight. Scientists estimate their survival on Earth at 10 million years. They migrate to the Greater Yellowstone Ecosystem in the spring and stay through the summer and early fall. The call of the sandhill is one of the most primitive and eeire in nature. They are officially considered by the Park Service to be uncommon in the area.

# Grand Teton National Park

*Ken McGraw*      *Nikon F3*      *Nikkor 600mm Lens, 1/500 sec. at f5.6*      *Tripod*      *64 Kodachrome*

### BULL MOOSE IN GRAND TETON NATIONAL PARK

On the morning this photograph was taken, two bulls were vying for the attention of a single cow. This male performs a flehmen posture after smelling the female.

Caution must be exercised when photographing in these circumstances because there is a flurry of unpredictable activity coming from all the animals.

The photographer of this picture went unnoticed because he stood near a tree with a long telephoto lens attached to his camera.

54

*Lorraine Salem Tufts    Canon T-90    Canon 24mm 2.8 Lens, 1/15 sec. at f16 with Polarizing Filter    Bogen Tripod    25 Kodachrome*

## GRAND TETON RANGE FROM OXBOW BEND

The ever-changing play of light, weather and position instills an endless desire to photograph the Grand Teton Range and the various bodies of water near them. This shot was taken on a cool summer morning with a wild member of the Sunflower Family in the foreground.

# The Geological Story

The Grand Teton Range is the youngest of all the Rocky Mountains. Nine million years ago, a north-south crack or fault of approximately 40 miles formed and extended along the foot of the mountains. East of the fault the surface dropped, while on the west side the earth tilted upward. This fault-block process forged the beginning of this magnificent range.

The rock that makes up the mountains is not young. It consists of granite gneisses and schists, formed 2.5 billion years ago, making this some of the oldest, hardest and least-porous rock in North America. About 1.3 billion years ago, dark igneous rock forced through the gneiss and granite, forming vertical dikes. One can easily be seen on the east face of Mount Moran.

A place to obtain a visual understanding of the fault line is from the flat plains to the east of the mountains. From this vantage point, the mountains virtually jut up from the valley floor. The peak of the Grand Teton exceeds 13,000 feet above sea level at 13,770 feet, while at least seven additional Teton peaks surpass heights of 12,000 feet. They are Mount Owen, Middle Teton, Mount Moran, South Teton, Teewinot Mountain, Thor Peak and Cloudveil Dome. In addition, there are many peaks which exceed 10,000 feet in this dramatic mountainscape.

Over time the valley block has dropped four times greater than the mountain mass has risen. The magnitude of this distance, however, is not evident from the Earth's surface because the valley block is covered by sedimentary debris.

The Earth uses many forces from within to sculpt her geological shape: pressure, heat, cracking and shifting. The story then continues with the outer forces called erosion — the wearing away of rock and soil by weathering, water flow, glaciers, and wind. Millions of years of rain fell, with water running down from the high places to the lower places, slowly wearing away and shaping the mountains.

This process continued until a cooling period occurred, (150,000 years ago) allowing snow to fall and accumulate, compact, and remain as ice. Again and again, the snow would fall, melt, and compact until these masses became enormous and very heavy. Gravity

*Brad Markel, Nikon F3 with Motor Drive, Nikkor 400mm 3.5 Lens, 1/250 sec. at f5.6, 64 Kodachrome*

## GRAY JAY

The play of light and tightness of the shot elevates this relatively familiar subject to visual glory. Note the detail of the loose, fluffy plumage which assists the gray jay in silent flight.

pulled them from their high mountain places. They moved great distances and carved the jagged appearance of the Teton Range. Over the thousands and thousands of years, more than one glacier did its work. Ice Age glaciers are responsible for shaping the mountains, carving the valleys and depositing soil, rock, and detritus in the lower valleys.

The last glacial advance, which ended fifteen thousand years ago, left five small, piedmont lakes at the foot of the eastern face of the mountains. Jenny, Bradley, Taggart , Leigh, and Phelps Lakes are held in by morainal dams. A moraine is a mound or ridge of massive rocks or sediment, unstratified in its character, and deposited chiefly by the direct action of glacial ice. The mountains and glacial lakes look very much the same today as they did at the end of the Ice Age.

Alpine glaciers are still supported by the mountains. They are nestled in north or east-facing cirques among the seven highest peaks. These mountain glaciers are not remnants from the Ice Age. They are only about 4,500 years old, originating from what is called the Little Ice Age. Although very small in comparison to the great glaciers of the major Ice Age, they continue to sculpt, carve, and grind the range.

Quartzite rock from glacial material covers the valley floor. This rock, mixed with gravel, sand, and silt, composes the soil which supports sagebrush, grasses, and other arid-adapted plants. Glacial runoff washed much of the clay content from this area, but lodgepole pines grow where the glacial moraines are younger and still rich in clay and nutrients. Water from lakes, rivers, streams, and ponds maintains willow bushes, spruce, and cottonwood trees.

The geological epic is long and detailed, spanning years of study and volumes of written material, yet a cursory look at this story can stimulate the curious and inform the laymen on how this breathtaking scenery was chiseled.

56

Henry H. Holdsworth          Nikon FM          Nikkor 55mm Lens, 1/60 sec. at f22          Bogen Tripod, Arca Swiss Mono Ball Head          64 Kodachrome

**GRAND TETON RANGE FROM THE SNAKE RIVER
OVERLOOK ON A WINTER MORNING**

# Man's History In Grand Teton

Just as the majestic peaks of the Grand Teton Range inspired the viewers of the past, they continue to instill a sense of awe to the visitors of the present. Because of the harsh winters and geographic isolation, the mountains remained cut off from the white man until the early 1800s. Even the nomadic Indian tribes, including the Bannock, Crow, Nez Pierce, Gros Ventre, and Shoshoni, who were natives of the area, could not tolerate the rigors of the Grand Teton winters.

In 1807 a fur trader named John Colter left the Lewis and Clark expedition to continue his search for fur-trading Indians. This search lead him to the Gros Ventre mountains from where he could see the Grand Teton Range, making him the first known white man to gaze upon these awesome peaks. Unfortunately, because Colter was a trapper and fur trader, he did not document any of his discoveries. The valley of the Grand Teton Range received its name, "Jackson's Hole," from Bill Sublette and "Davey" Jackson who, like Colter, preferred to trap in this area. By the 1840s, however, the various trappers and explorers began to leave the region, and not until forty years later did people begin to settle the region permanently. A U.S. government survey expedition involving some of the most prominent explorers began in 1872. Artist Thomas Moran captured in his sketches the beauty and reality of the mountains. U.S. geologist F.J. Bradley and his assistant, W.R. Taggart, gathered scientific data, and the legendary guide, Richard Leigh, better known as "Beaver Dick," successfully led the group through the area.

Many of the permanent settlers of the late 1880s included groups of varying interests. The cattlemen wanted to protect the grazing land from sheep; other concerned settlers wanted to protect the elk and other wildlife from profit-seeking hunters as well as sportsmen. There were also those that had an ability to recognize potentially long-term problems. Some men began to worry that the influx of people would alter the ecosystem to such an extent that the environment would suffer irreparable damages. Already changes had occurred which had caused a breakdown in the food chain of the wandering elk herds. Unfortunately, the need to preserve this area's wildlife did not become a public issue until 1918, and not until 1929 did Congress vote to create a Grand Teton National Park.

One of the most successful men to carry out this desire to preserve the Teton wilderness was John D. Rockefeller. The deep concerns of Horace Albright, Superintendent of Yellowstone National Park, and a handful of concerned residents of Jackson Hole stirred a dream in Rockefeller's soul which prompted him to safeguard the land from commercialization and various other forms of exploitation. Through a land company, Rockefeller slowly acquired vast portions of the Jackson Valley. Although the years were tumultuous and difficult, he and his family continued to achieve this goal.

President Franklin D. Roosevelt established by proclamation the Jackson Hole National Monument to contain those lands purchased by Rockefeller. In 1950 the monument lands were added to the Grand Teton National Park.

Because of the overwhelming beauty and appeal of the Grand Teton Range, the exploration and desire to preserve the region became a personal goal for many. These individuals hoped that all people would recognize our dependence on as well as the intrinsic value of nature. They understood man's relatively fragile and young existence within nature and therefore insisted that our nation not try to conquer the environment, but instead try to live in harmony with it. They understood that if man preserved the environment, he would also preserve his place in it.

**57**

*Henry H. Holdsworth     Nikon FM     Nikkor 28mm Lens, 1/30 sec. at f22     Gitzo Tripod     64 Kodachrome*

**THE GRAND TETON RANGE
FROM AN OLD CABIN**

58

*Neil and Trish Ramhorst    Nikon FE2    Nikkor 400mm 3.5 Lens, 1/60 sec. at f3.5  64 Kodachrome*

## CINNAMON COLORED BLACK BEAR WITH CARRION

Animal carcasses from the winter kill are an important food source for bears in the early spring.  This bear was feeding while alarmed by another black bear watching in a tree.  A long, fast telephoto lens was necessary to create this photograph.  Although black bears are not as aggressive as grizzly bears, approaching this situation is dangerous at best and should be avoided.

*Lorraine Salem Tufts      Canon EOS      Canon300mm
2.8 lens, 1/500 at f5.6                         100 Fujichrome*

*Lorraine Salem Tufts      Canon T-90      Canon300mm
2.8 lens, 1/500 at f5.6                         64 Kodachrome.*

## COTTONTAIL AND GROUND SQUIRREL

Cottontails and ground squirrels reproduce in great numbers.  Grizzly bears and black bears catch and eat rodents and rabbits when they can.  Nature has a part for each of them to play in the circle of life on Earth.

*Brad Markel*　　　　*Nikon F3 with Motor Drive*　　　　*Nikkor 400mm 3.5 Lens, 1/125 sec. at f5.6*　　　　*Tripod*　　　　*64 Kodachrome*

### GRIZZLY BEAR WITH HER CUBS

Getting between a grizzly bear sow and her cubs can be one of the most dangerous situations for humans and animals in the park. Give the bears a great deal of room and retreat as slowly and as calmly as possible.

*Lorraine Salem Tufts*  *Canon T-90*  *Canon 150-600mm Lens, 1/350 sec. at f5.6*  *Bogen Tripod*  *200 Kodachrome*

### KIT RED FOX JUST OUTSIDE THE DEN

Photographing fox is very difficult because they are so secretive and there are not many around.

Although this fox is called "red," they come in many colors such as reddish-brown, reddish-gold, brownish-yellow, silver-tipped mixed with pure black, and black. These different colorations all share the usual characteristic of the white tail tip.

This photograph was taken in the Greater Yellowstone Ecosystem with the vixen close by. The photographer used stillness and a natural blind as her allies.

*Lorraine Salem Tufts*          *Canon T-90*          *Canon 85-300mm 4.5 Lens, 1/500 sec. at f4.5*          *Monopod*          *200 Kodachrome*

## C O Y O T E   P O U N C I N G   O N   A   M E A D O W   V O L E

Coyotes are graceful hunters, capturing small rodents and other prey with quick leaps or pounces. They are invaluable for controlling rodent populations throughout Grand Teton and Yellowstone National Parks. Highly respected by many naturalists, the coyote has earned admiration for its unyielding resilience to survive.

62

*Neil Ramhorst      Nikon FE2      Nikkor 200mm Lens, 1/125 sec. at f8 2/3      64 Kodachrome*

*Trish Ramhorst                                                                 Nikon FE2*
*Nikkor 300mm Lens, 1/125 sec. at f8 2/3              Gitzo Tripod              64 Kodachrome*

## LONG-TAILED WEASELS

Long-tailed weasels are the largest of all weasels. Males are larger than females, weighing as much as nine ounces. Their summer pelage is brown on top and yellowish underneath. In winter, they turn white to blend with the snow.

The second photograph shows a standing weasel looking out over the glacier lilies.

*Lorraine Salem Tufts*     *Canon T-90*     *Canon 35-105mm 3.5 Lens, 1/90 sec. at f22, Polarizing Filter*     *Cullman Tripod*     *100 Fujichrome*

## JENNY LAKE AND MOUNT TEEWINOT

Jenny Lake is the result of glacial ice, flowing from the canyons of the Tetons, which created a basin-formed lake. Similarly, Leigh, Bradley, Taggart, and Phelps Lakes, often called the little jewels of the park, are glacial lakes. In the background Mount Teewinot rises overhead at 12,325 feet.

**64**

*Lorraine Salem Tufts*  *Canon F1 with Motor Drive*  *Canon 600mm Lens, 1/60 sec. at f5.6*  *Bogen Tripod*  *64 Kodachrome*

**BULL ELK BUGLING DURING THE RUT**

*Lorraine Salem Tufts*
*Canon 35-105mm Lens, 1/60 sec. at f5.6*

*Canon T-90*
*64 Kodachrome*

## COW MOOSE WITH CALVES

Moose are the least sociable of all members of the deer family, although a mother moose is very attentive to her calves. Renowned for her protective tendencies, she is seen here sizing up a group of curious park visitors.

The photographer caught the calves in an amusing position as they attempt to stand.

*Lorraine Salem Tufts*
*Canon 300mm 2.8 Lens, 1/500 sec. at f5.6*

*Canon T-90*
*64 Kodachrome*

## COW MOOSE WITH CALVES NURSING

*Lorraine Salem Tufts*
*Canon 35-105mm Lens, 1/60 sec. at f9.5, Polarizing Filter*

*Canon T-90*
*100 Fujichrome*

## HIDDEN FALLS

The hike to Hidden Falls is short and popular, but the 250 foot drop of the falls is well worth the effort. It is an ascending hike with glacier-polished rocks, green forests, marmots, other wildlife and the sounds of rushing water.

*Lorraine Salem Tufts*   *Canon F1 with Motor Drive*   *Canan 150-600mm 5.6 zoom Lens, 1/125 sec. at f5.6*   *Gitzo Tripod*   *64 Kodachrome*

## BISON YAWNING

This photograph was taken during the height of the rut, yet this young bison was undisturbed by all the activities.

Bison males usually do not mate until their fifth year when they are strong enough to dominate other males. Females are receptive to breeding by their second year.

68

*C. F. Glover*          *Canon F1*          *Canon 70-210mm 4.0 Zoom Lens, 1/125 sec. at f11*          *Zone VI Wood Tripod, Cable Release*          *Fujichrome 100*

## MOUNT MORAN AT MOONSET AND SUNRISE

The only way to obtain a photograph like this one is to rise very early, dress very warmly, and keep the camera warm to avoid battery problems. Moonset over the Grand Teton Range during a winter sunrise is spectacular subject matter to capture on film.

*Neil and Trish Ramhorst*
*Nikkor 500mm Lens, 1/500 sec. at f5.6 1/2*          *Gitzo Tripod*          *Nikon F2AS*
*64 Kodachrome*

## IMMATURE BALD EAGLE

After five years of seasonal molting, the bald eagle gradually evolves a snow white head, neck, and tail. It also develops a yellow bill from the brownish-yellow one of its youth.

*Lorraine Salem Tufts*
*Canon 600mm 4Lens, 1/500 sec. at f5.6*      *Bogen Tripod*

*Canon EOS A2E*
*100 Fujichrome*

## RED-TAILED HAWK IN FLGHT

This is one of the largest hawks in the ecosystem. It hunts by soaring or perching in a tree, where it can use its excellent vision to spot the slightest movement of its potential prey. Red-tailed hawks can dive at speeds of 120 miles per hour, snatching a snake or rodent with precision.

*Lorraine Salem Tufts*
*Canon 150-600mm Lens, 1/500 sec. at f5.6*      *Bogen Tripod*

*Canon T -90*
*64 Kodachrome*

## OSPREY FEEDING HER YOUNG

The female osprey does most of the incubation of the eggs while the male fishes for his mate. A mated pair have an admirable working relationship that usually lasts until one dies.

*Ken McGraw      Nikon F3      Nikkor 43-86mm Lens, 1/125 sec. at f5.6      64 Kodachrome*

### IMMATURE RED-TAILED HAWK ON THE NEST

Buteos are hawks of the plains, open woodlands, fields, and mountains. Their diet consists mainly of rodents; however, red-tailed hawks will kill snakes, skunks, lizards, and other ground-dwelling prey. The nest of this five-week-old immature and its parents showed evidence of chipmunk, rabbit, and even marmot remains surrounding it.

72

*Lorraine Salem Tufts*     *Canon EOS A2E*     *Canon 600mm 4 Lens, 1/500 sec. at f5.6*     *Bogen Tripod with Wimberly Head Mount*     *Fuji Provia 100*

## MALE AMERICAN KESTREL

Considered a real beauty in all its colors, markings and proportion, this small hawk is about nine to 12 inches in length. The male has blue-gray wings and head; a buff breast and nape, and rufous, or rusty crown, back and tail with black markings. Although a little less colorful the female is also striking. They eat mostly insects and small rodents. The male often helps with incubation during nesting, which is unusual in raptors.

*Lorraine Salem Tufts*          *Canon EOS 5*          *Canon 28-105 mm Lens, 1/2 sec. at f22*
*Bogen Tripod*          *Polarizing Filter*          *Kodak E100VS*

## THE TETON RANGE DURING THE FALL COLORS WITH A MIRRORED REFLECTION

On a clear day the Tetons can be seen from 150 miles in every direction. In the 1800's Canadian fur trappers approaching from the west named the three tallest peaks they saw, "Les Trois Tetons!" the three breast. From the center to the left they are Grand Teton, Middle Teton and South Teton. These three peaks with Mount Owen and Mount Teewinot to the right comprise the Cathedral Group

74

*Lorraine Salem Tufts*          *Canon T-90*          *Canon 150-600mm Lens, 1/500 sec. at f5.6*          *Bogen Tripod*          *50 Fuji Velvia*

## WHITE PELICAN FISHING AT SUNSET

The contrast of light and dark does more than register subject matter. It creates a mood.

White pelicans fish while they swim on the surface of a lake or stream. They virtually scoop fish into their large pouch. Beautiful in flight, these are extremely large birds with a wing span often as wide as nine feet.

Great care must be exercised to insure their safety and tranquility during nesting and caring for their young.

*Ken McGraw*          *Nikon F3*          *Nikkor 300mm Lens, 1/500 sec. at f5.6*          *Gitzo Tripod*          *64 Kodachrome*

## CANADA GEESE WITH GOSLINGS

Canada geese are usually migratory, yet many spend the winter in the Grand Teton and Yellowstone National Parks. These geese mate for life and courtship begins in April. Both adult geese share the responsibilities of caring for the young. The gander drives off intruders while the goose incubates the eggs in the nest. Geese eat vegetation from streams and lakes, in addition to grass and other grazing foods. During the nesting season, the adults go into a molt and are unable to fly for approximately three weeks. Immediately after hatching, the goslings are able to swim and feed themselves. The adults, however, will not leave their sides until the goslings can fly.

*Lorraine Salem Tufts*          *Canon EOS A2E*          *Canon 300mm 2.8 Lens, 1/500 sec. at f4*          *Monopod*          *64Kodachrome*

### TRUMPETER SWAN IN FLIGHT
In 1933 it was believed that only about 70 remained in the lower 48 States, all in and around the Greater Yellowstone Ecosystem. Before that time they were primarily killed for meat and feathers, and their skin was used to make powder puffs. Today the trumpeter swan has made a comeback due to conservation efforts. The male is called a cob, the female a pen, and the young are called cygnets.

*Lorraine Salem Tufts*          *Canon T-90*          *Canon 150-600mm Lens, 1/500 sec. at f5.6*          *Bogen Tripod*          *64 Kodachrome*

## A PAIR OF TRUMPETER SWANS

Grand Teton and Yellowstone support the largest of waterfowl. Grace and elegance best describe the movement of the trumpeter swan.

Once nearly extinct, these swans are struggling to maintain a stable population. They need special conditions for breeding and a lot of privacy. Great care must be taken when photographing trumpeter swans. A small infraction could become a major problem for this species.

78

*Lorraine Salem Tufts*     *Canon T-90*     *300mm 2.8 Lens, 1/500 sec. at f8*     *Pillow Mount*     *100 Fujichrome*

### GREAT BLUE HERON

The great blue heron wades in shallow water, waiting patiently for unsuspecting fish, frogs, snakes and other aquatic life small enough for it to swallow. The heron featured in this picture leaped into flight during excellent light, making an exceptional composition for the photographer's picture.

Once great blue herons have survived their first year, they can have a long life, usually ten years, and sometimes spanning up to fifteen or twenty years.

*Al Buchanan*　　　　　*Olympus OM1*　　　　　*Zuiko 40mm Lens, 1/250 sec. at f16*　　　　　*64 Kodachrome*

## LAKE SOLITUDE

Lake Solitude cannot be photographed without a 7.2-mile hike from the west shore boat dock on Jenny Lake. The Hidden Falls Foot Trail starts near there and leads to Cascade Canyon, to the Forks of Cascade Creek, and finally to Lake Solitude. Along the way, a view of Hidden Falls, Inspiration Point, glacial moraines, Teewinot Mountain, Grand Teton, Mount Owen, and Cascade Canyon's glacial sculpturing can all be enjoyed and studied. Also worth mentioning are the wild flowers, pikas, marmots and white crowned sparrows.

Overnight camping is not permitted at Lake Solitude, so it is best to discuss your course of action with a Park Ranger before attempting this adventure.

80

*Lorraine Salem Tufts*                                    *Canon EOS A2E*
*Canon 35-350mm 3.5-5.6 Lens, 1/60 sec. at f5.6*          *Fuji Sensia 100*

## MALE MOUNTAIN BLUEBIRD
Its rich blue plumage is splendid to behold.

*C. F. Glover*                                            *Canon F1 with Motor Drive*
*Canon 70-210mm Macro Zoom Lens on a 25mm Tube, 1/500 sec. at f11*
*Homemade Electronic Cable Release, Zone VI Wood Tripod*          *200 Kodachrome*

## FEMALE HUMMINGBIRD
Calliope, broad-tailed, rufous, black-chinned and rivoli's hummingbirds have all been seen in Grand Teton National Park. Yellowstone lists rare sightings of calliope, broad-tailed and rufous hummingbirds.

*Lorraine Salem Tufts*
*Canon 300mm 2.8 Lens, with 2x teleconverter, 1/250 sec. at f5.6 Monopod*

*Canon EOS A2E*
*Fuji Sensia 100*

## SANDHILL CRANE COLT

This young colt seems as curious as the observer. The long lens and a quiet, stationary photographer crouching on the ground for hours seemed non-threatening to the adult sandhill cranes and of great interest to the chick. A colt, or chick, will stay with its parents for about 10 months, but will fledge in two.

*Ken McGraw*
*Nikkor 55mm Macro Lens, 1/60 sec. at f8*　　　*Portable Flash*　　　*Nikon F3*
*64 Kodachrome*

## ROBIN'S EGGS HATCHING

This nest was just four feet off the ground and built into the pocket of a cottonwood tree. The mother robin was incubating four blue eggs the first time the nest was discovered. After a few days, three of the babies were emerging from the eggs.

Different species of birds have varied levels of tolerance to human intrusion around the nesting site. Knowledge about the individual species can avoid pressure on the nesting birds.

*Lorraine Salem Tufts*    *Canon EOS 5*    *Canon 300 mm 2.8 Lens, w/2x extender, 1/250 sec. at f5.6*
*Monopod*                                                                    *Fuji Provia100*

## GREAT HORNED OWL

Although common in all of North America it is a pleasure seeing this large owl in the early morning light. Standing 18 to 25 inches. Great horned owls hunt rabbits, mice, crows, ducks, other owls and even skunks. Many rodents and birds fall prey to this nocturnal raptor.

*Lorraine Salem Tufts    EOS A2E    Canon 35-350mm 3.5 Lens, 1/250 sec. at f5.6    100 Fujichrome*

## BLACK BEAR STRETCHING FOR BERRIES

Crawling up a flimsy tree is an easy task for hungry black bears looking for berries in late summer and fall. Service berries, chokecherries and other varieties are available. When the harvest is plentiful they eat until full, retreat back into the forest perhaps for a rest, returning again in late afternoon. They must compete with other bears and animals for the sweet fruit of the season and competition can be tough at times.

*Lorraine Salem Tufts*
*Canon 300 mm Lens, 1/30sec at f2.8*          *Monopod*          *Canon EOS 5*
*Fugi Provia100*

## BLUE GROUSE MALE

*Lorraine Salem Tufts*
*Canon 35-30 mm 2.8 Lens, 1/60 sec. with flash*          *Canon EOS A2E*
*Fuji Provia100*

## BLUE GROUSE FEMALE

The male is impressive when displaying his courting rituals. Especially noticeable are the orange-yellow combs over the eyes and the purplish pouches on either side of his neck. The courtship display is imposing with "booms" sounding by the inflation and deflation of his pouches. The female is mottled brown with a dark tail.

*Lorraine Salem Tufts*                    *Canon EOS 5*
*Canon 300 mm 2.8 Lens, 1/500 sec. at f5.6*

**P I K A**

*Lorraine Salem Tufts*                    *Canon EOS 5*
*Canon 600 mm 4. Lens, 1/125 sec. at f4*
*Bogen Tripod*                    *Fuji Provia100*

**B E A V E R**

*Lorraine Salem Tufts*                    *Canon EOS A2E*
*Canon 600 mm 4. Lens, 1/500 sec. at f4*
*Bogen Tripod*                    *Fuji Provia100*

**B A R R O W ' S   G O L D E N E Y E**
**M A L E   A N D   F E M A L E**

*Lorraine Salem Tufts*                    *Canon EOS A2E*
*Canon 600 mm 4. Lens, 1/500 sec. at f4*
*Bogen Tripod*                    *Fuji Provia100*

**Y E L L O W H E A D E D   B L A C K B I R D**

*Lorraine Salem Tufts*
*Bogen Tripod*

*Canon EOS 5*
*Polarizing Filter*

*Canon 28-105 mm Lens, 1/15 sec. at f16*
*Fuji Velvia 50*

**REFLECTIONS OF COTTONWOOD TREES ON THE SNAKE RIVER IN THE FALL**

88

*Lorraine Salem Tufts*  *Canon EOS A2E*  *Canon 20-35 mm Lens, 1/2 sec. at f22*  *Bogen Tripod*  *Polarizing Filter*  *Fuji Velvia 50*

**EARLY MORNING LIGHT ON THE GRAND TETON RANGE WITH A
MIRRORED REFLECTION OF THE SNOW COVERED PEAKS AND
THE FALL COLORS OF THE TREES**

# Fire & Regrowth

## IMAGES FROM THE 1988 FIRES IN THE GREATER YELLOWSTONE AREA

Photographs by LORRAINE SALEM TUFTS

*Smoke billows over Yellowstone Lake near Grant Village.*

*Fire destroys signs and trees along the road at West Thumb.*

*Most animals instinctively move away from the threat of fire.*

*A conflagration can create its own weather.*

*Fire burns through the night.*

*25,000 fire fighters and 117 aircraft worked on the fires.*

The Greater Yellowstone Area consists of two National Parks and parts of six National Forests. This area drew the largest fire suppression effort ever undertaken in the United States. The fires of 1988 created more national attention in the area than any other event in its history.

90

**S U N S E T   D U R I N G   A   F I R E   S E A S O N**

**S M O K E   O V E R   Y E L L O W S T O N E   L A K E**

In response to the 1988 fires, two independent teams of land managers and scientists were appointed by the secretaries of the interior and agriculture and by the National Park Service to assess aspects of fire management and control in the Yellowstone area. The two groups, the Fire Management Policy Review Team and the Greater Yellowstone Area Post-Fire Ecological Assessment Panel both concluded that "some kind of natural-fire program, in which lightning-caused fires are allowed to burn under certain conditions, is appropriate and necessary for maintaining the wilderness value of parks and other refuges."

The Christensen report, submitted by the Greater Yellowstone Area Panel, further emphasized the fact that although large fires have burned in the past, this fact alone does not legitimize their existence today. This is because our wilderness areas are much smaller and more confined than they used to be.

Young forests, which replace those burned only a few years previously, usually experience a great diversity of species. In fact, certain species seem to thrive after the event of a fire. Purple fireweed and other herbaceous species are often the first to grow on the floor of a recently burned forest. Moisture is needed to assist in the rapid growth of species. Those areas which are less moist and fertile may follow those with more moisture by several years.

*Henry H. Holdsworth*
*w/2x teleconverter, 1/250 sec. at f11*

*Canon EOS3*
*Gitzo Tripod*

*Canon 300mm 2.8 Lens*
*Fuji Provia 100*

## THREE WOLVES ON A SUNNY WINTER'S DAY

In 1995 and 1996 gray wolves were reintroduced in Yellowstone National Park. Thirty-one wolves were moved from Canada in those two years. The leading biologists of the program are astounded with the success so far. Gray wolves travel in packs and as loners through both Yellowstone and Grand Teton National Parks.

*Henry H. Holdsworth*
*teleconverter, 1/250 sec. at f8*

*Canon EOS 3*
*Gitzo Tipod*

*Canon 600mm 4 Lens, with2x*
*Fuji Provia 100*

## FEMALE MOUNTAIN LION WITH PLAYFUL KITTENS

Few people ever see mountain lions in the wild, because they are very quiet and more active at night. What a thrill for the lucky onlookers who saw these three in the Greater Yellowstone Ecosystem.

# The Greater Yellowstone Ecosystem

"The Earth does not belong to man; man belongs to the Earth... Man did not weave the web of life, he is merely a strand in it. Whatever he does to the web, he does to himself." These words are credited to Chief Seatlh of the Swuamish Tribe. The Native American had a reverence for preserving the Earth, and he and his people lived it. White men seem reluctant to accept this thought, even with more and more documented evidence of endangered species and animal extinction in our country. Aldo Leopold addressed the problem in 1949 when he wrote, "We abuse land because we regard it as a commodity belonging to us. When we see land as a community to which we belong, we may begin to use it with love and respect."

Our young nation found it difficult to imagine that nature would be finite. With millions and millions of acres to consume, there was no thought of the greater picture. The near extinction of the bison exemplifies this misunderstanding.

The thoughts and philosophies of a man like John Muir were unusual, and yet in the mid 1800s, President Abraham Lincoln had the foresight to sign a bill appointing jurisdiction over Yosemite Valley to the state of California. Theodore Roosevelt also pointed out "that a nation is obligated to manage its resources for the greater good of the greatest number over the long run."

Each of these men and others like them carried the spirit of the Earth in their souls, each passing the torch to the next generation. And yet, it seems something was lost in the transition, because our natural world is dwindling, and it is mostly man-induced. Destroying or distorting one part of the natural world can trigger a chain reaction which takes years to discover, trace back, and solve. Sometimes, the remedy arrives too late.

Today, there is an awareness that Yellowstone and Grand Teton National Parks need more space to protect the wildlife. The Greater Yellowstone Ecosystem is becoming a common term among conservationists, scientists, park officials, and, hopefully, the general public. The term *ecosystem* means the result of interactions between the Earth's biological, chemical, and physical systems. The Greater Yellowstone Ecosystem comprises the two parks, surrounding national forests, various wildlife refuges, and other federal, state and private lands, yet the protection of wildlife and the land is incomplete. The grizzly bear, trumpeter swan, bison, white pelican, coyote, bald eagle, bobcat, elk, black bear, and other species need the safety of the whole ecosystem to prosper. Careful studies, unhampered ancient migration routes, various nesting areas, undisturbed habitat and certain plant and animal availability are imperative for the true stewardship of the area.

Yellowstone, once an area just for witnessing thermal activities, has slowly become one of the last habitats for certain species. This message from nature cannot be ignored. It must be studied, contemplated, and argued to a workable solution.

Our nation's land philosophy once advocated use and dispose, but is gradually turning toward an attitude of learning to conserve, preserve, and replace. Scientific principles should manage the ecosystem and preserve scenic wonders with the protection of law. This can help our commitment to retain this natural world for the enjoyment of future generations of human and wildlife inhabitants.

Lorraine Salem Tufts          Canon T-90          Canon 35-105mm Lens, 1/250 sec. at f8          64 Kodachrome

**THE GRAY WOLF**

## ADDITIONAL READINGS

**LEOPOLD, ALDO.** *A Sand County Almanac.* Oxford University Press, New York. 1947.

**HAINES, AUBREY L.** *The Yellowstone Story.* Yellowstone Library & Museum Association in cooperation with Colorado Associated University Press, Yellowstone National Park. 1977.

**FOLLETT, DICK.** *Birds Of Yellowstone,* Roberts Rinehart, Inc., Boulder. 1988.

**LEE, WELDON.** *Photographing Rocky Mountain Wildlife,* Westcliffe Publishers, Englewood, Colorado. 1996.

**PETERSON, ROGER TORY.** *A Field Guide To Western Birds.* Houghton Mifflin Company, Boston. 1990.

**UDVARDY, MIKLOS D. F.** *The Audubon Society Field Guide To North American Birds.* Alfred A. Knopf, New York. 1977.

**BURT, WILLIAM H. & RICHARD P. GROSSENHEIDER,** *Peterson Field Guides: Mammals.* Houghton Mifflin Company, New York. 1980.

**MC FARLAND, DAVID.** *The Oxford Companion to Animal Behavior.* Oxford University Press, New York. 1987.

**CHITTENDEN, HIRAM M.** *The Yellowstone National Park.* University of Oklahoma Press, Norman and London. New Edition 1964,

**FULLER, STEVEN & JEREMY SCHMIDT.** *Yellowstone In Three Seasons.* Snow Country Publications, Yellowstone. 1980.

**HARRY, BRYRON & WILLARD E. DILLEY.** *Wildlife Of Yellowstone and Grand Teton National Parks.* Wheelwright Press Ltd., Salt Lake City. 1972.

**JOHNSON, SYLVIA A. & ALICE AAMODT.** *Wolf Pack Tracking Wolves in the Wild.* Lerner Publications Company, Minneapolis. 1985.

**FISCHER, HANK.** *Wolf Wars.* Falcon Press Publishing Co., Inc. Helena and Billings. 1995.

**HALFPENNY, JAMES. & ELIZABETH BIESIOT.** *A Field Guide to Mammal Tracking in North America.* Johnson Publishing Company. Boulder. 1987.

**SCHREIER, CARL.** *A Field Guide To Yellowstone's Geysers, Hot Springs and Fumaroles.* Homestead Publishing. Moose, Wy. 1987.

**HENRY, JEFF.** *Yellowstone Winter Guide.* Roberts Rindhart Publishers. Niwot, Co. 1993.

**FRITZ, WILLIAM J.** *Roadside Geology Of The Yellowstone Country.* Roadside Geology Series, Mountain Press Publishing Company. Missoula. 1989.

**WHITTLESEY, LEE H.** *Yellowstone Place Names.* Montana Historical Society Press, Helena. 1988.

C. F. Glover    Canon AE1P    Canon 70-210mm Lens, 1/250 sec. at f8    Bogen Tripod    64 Kodachrome

**"THE GRAND" FROM ANTELOPE FLATS**

We hope you've enjoyed
*Secrets in Yellowstone &*
*Grand Teton National Parks.*

If you would like additional copies
of this book, other books or prod-
ucts, please use the attached order
forms or call our toll free number
within the USA at 1-800-411-6144
or visit our website at:
www.NationalPhotoCollections.com

Thank you.

---

**NATIONAL PHOTOGRAPHIC COLLECTIONS**

O R D E R   F O R M

**Secrets in Yellowstone & Grand Teton National Parks**

1. Hardcover $29.95 x _____ (quantity) = _____

2. Softcover  $19.95 x _____ (quantity) = _____

**Secrets in the Grand Canyon, Zion
and Bryce Canyon National Parks**

3. Hardcover $29.95 x _____ (quantity) = _____

4. Softcover  $19.95 x _____ (quantity) = _____

**Animals in Action**

5. Hardcover $15.95 x _____ (quantity) = _____

Shipping & Handling for 1 book

   U.S. and Canada      $5.50.

   Outside the U.S.     $15.00.

Each additional book add    $2.00 x _____ = _____

Add 6% sales tax for Florida shipments:  _____

                            **Total due**    _____

☐ **Please advise me of future publications**

Purchaser _____

Address _____

City _____ State_____ Zip_____

Phone (_____)_____

☐ **Ship to (if different than above)**

Name _____

Address _____

City _____ State_____ Zip_____

*Please enclose check, money orders or Visa Card number:*
Card # _____
Expiration: _____

National Photographic Collections
390F Golfview Road, North Palm Beach, Fl.
33408-3570

---

**NATIONAL PHOTOGRAPHIC COLLECTIONS**

O R D E R   F O R M

**Secrets in Yellowstone & Grand Teton National Parks**

1. Hardcover $29.95 x _____ (quantity) = _____

2. Softcover  $19.95 x _____ (quantity) = _____

**Secrets in the Grand Canyon, Zion
and Bryce Canyon National Parks**

3. Hardcover $29.95 x _____ (quantity) = _____

4. Softcover  $19.95 x _____ (quantity) = _____

**Animals in Action**

5. Hardcover $15.95 x _____ (quantity) = _____

Shipping & Handling for 1 book

   U.S. and Canada      $5.50.

   Outside the U.S.     $15.00.

Each additional book add    $ 2.00 x _____ = _____

Add 6% sales tax for Florida shipments:  _____

                            **Total due**    _____

☐ **Please advise me of future publications**

Purchaser _____

Address _____

City _____ State_____ Zip_____

Phone (_____)_____

☐ **Ship to (if different than above)**

Name _____

Address _____

City _____ State_____ Zip_____

*Please enclose check, money orders or Visa Card number:*
Card # _____
Expiration: _____

National Photographic Collections
390F Golfview Road, North Palm Beach, Fl.
33408-3570